Harvest Moon

Nicole Engen

BookLeaf Publishing

India | USA | UK

Presentation by *BookLeaf Publishing*

Web: www.bookleafpub.com

E-mail: info@bookleafpub.com

ISBN: 9789358315578

First edition 2024

Dedicated to my Mom,

who always lights my candle.

Waning Gibbous

the goddesses protect her in three,
though men have wielded their silver swords
for being victims there are no awards,
women may rage like the Black Sea
so inner peace she must venture towards…
the goddesses!

from narcissism remain an absentee,
release the patient and sage the wards
that restrained; she barely affords
to think less of herself, she cannot flee
the goddesses.

Heart for a Heart

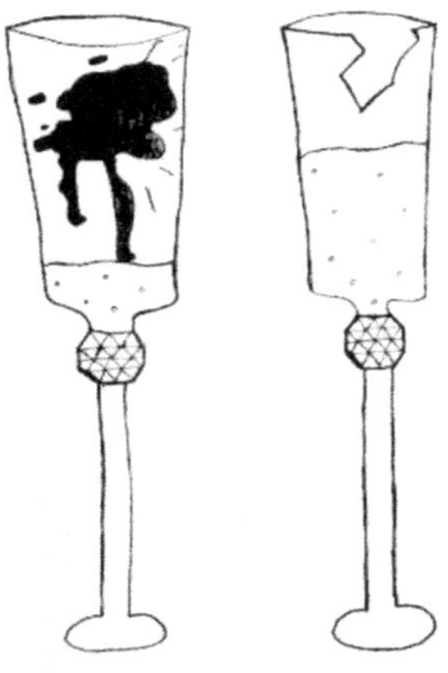

blood on her wedding veil,
the bridesmaids begin to wail
at the moon to no avail,
vlad the impaler has slain;
broken glasses of champagne,
the groom now a bloody stain
of gory guts and brain
on her silk dress.
a widow screeches in distress,
my my, what a mess
made in the name of love,
or lack thereof,
what he was deprived of
he steals from his true love.

Killer Gaze

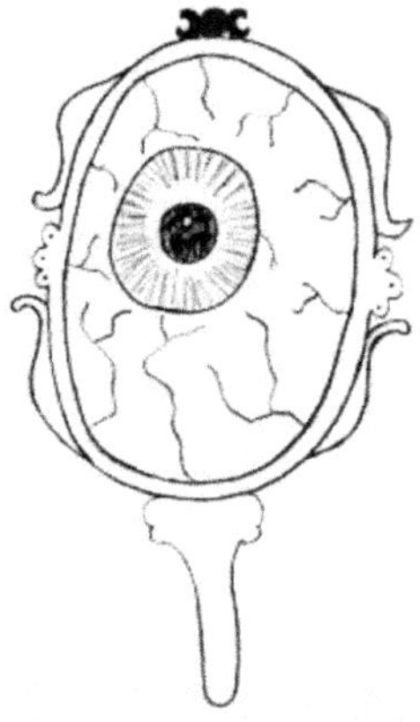

she silently brushes her hair
which curls in protest of the act,
but with her hair she has a pact
to hear the hissing in the air,
terrified another might stare,
or worse, at the temple there sat
a seducer ready to chat
but heaven forbid seduction,
so to honor this reduction,
she prayed for nothing to look at.

To Be Frank

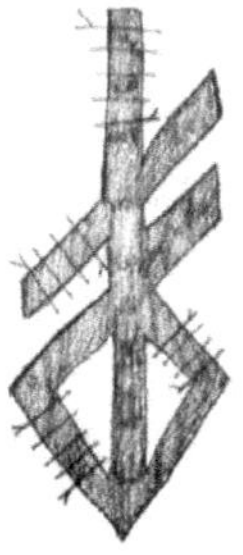

madness and science both,
he took a scalpel with an oath,
stitch with life,
but greed ran rife,
eyes stare back with reproach.

Last Quarter

he remains sharp like the star has five
points piercing through the loss of golden cups
that once overflowed, but gold corrupts,
and now in the storm of being alive,
when the planets align and he erupts,
he remains sharp.

gazing at the tower, to revive
something now fallen is to see the ups
amongst the downs, disillusion disrupts
the ability to heal; so while he must survive
he remains sharp.

Holy Ghost!

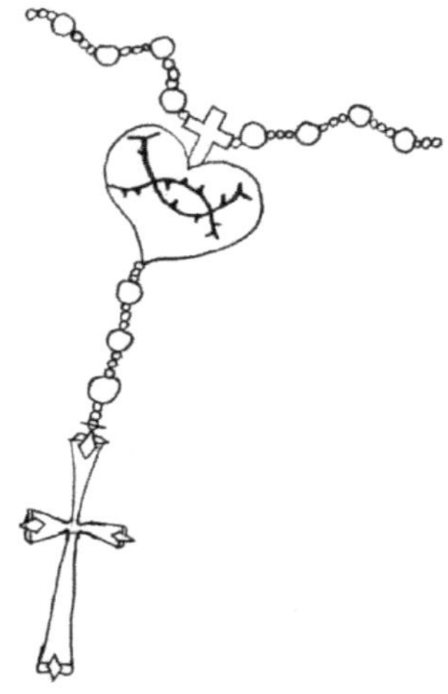

golden shards of a stained glass window
pierce his skin to draw ruby drops,
the church bell ringing suddenly stops
golden shards of a stained glass window.

pierce his skin to draw ruby drops,
a chilling whisper induces goosebumps
as he drops his rosary and jumps,
pierce his skin to draw ruby drops.

a chilling whisper induces goosebumps

while the choir hums a holy tune,
perhaps a warning but he is immune,
a chilling whisper induces goosebumps.

while the choir hums a holy tune,
wails of the deceased shake the cross
that hangs in the shadows of loss,
while the choir hums a holy tune.

golden shards of a stained glass window
pierce his skin to draw ruby drops,
the church bell ringing suddenly stops
golden shards of a stained glass window.

Oh Amoratus

with eyes like deadly nightshade
and a breath
as gentle as the hug from sweet,
sweet belladonna;
hail the queen
of serpentine
whose feet grace the water,
whose honey-coated whisper beckons
the lost souls
aching,
howling
for a forever rest that may be induced
by fang, should the fang present itself,
ooze poison from itself; she knows.
she knows you need a break,
when you cry it out to the skies
above Corytophanidae,
she will answer.
oh, Amoratus.

Fate Mummified

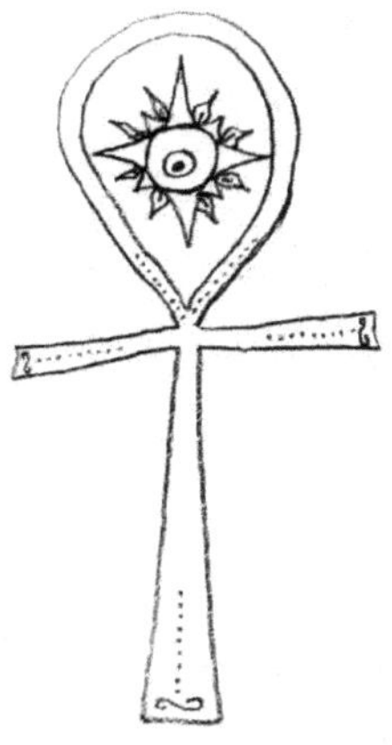

hieroglyphics carved into stone,
a pharaoh of preservation
wraps linen for restoration,
life after death may be unknown,
jewels and riches will not atone
but copper tools sculpt the story.
buried with more than their glory,
the Nile rushes more than death
that follows the sandy last breath,
wrapping up a life so gory.

Waning Crescent

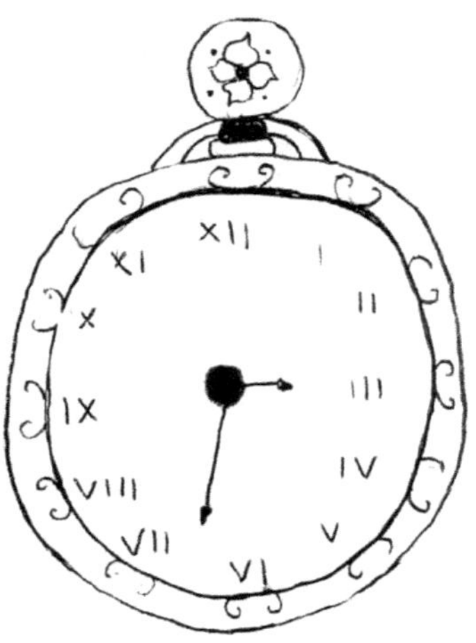

the lion's roar echoes at three
in the afternoon, with sticks like wands
atop the cliff, their shared strength bonds
the man and his strategy to see
the world, with his hunger corresponds
the lion's roar.

strong above all else, he is truly free
from the chains of indecision responds
the ebb and flow of tides in the ponds;
reborn from mars, rebirth will guarantee
the lion's roar.

A Braw Night in the Highlands

the eerie vines reek of death
with their blue tinge,
like the lips of a person horrifically suffocating
with eyes bulging brighter
than the eyes of her,
lurking, leering,
deciding whether it was time
for a snack or meal.
the vines did not dare strangle
his soft neck, skin not yet shredded,

as though not to spoil
her meal.
she was ready
to maul.
the night then consumed the loch
with shadows cackling,
vines left torn and dangling,
clinging on to dear life
like he so dearly tried.

Wolf? Where?

a snarl, a growl, a howl,
sing to the trees of pine
that quiver at night,
a full moon reveals
this inner beast of mine.

gray fur matted with blood
stains of something feral,
senses so heightened,
the fear tangible,
thick fog brims with peril.

Cranberry

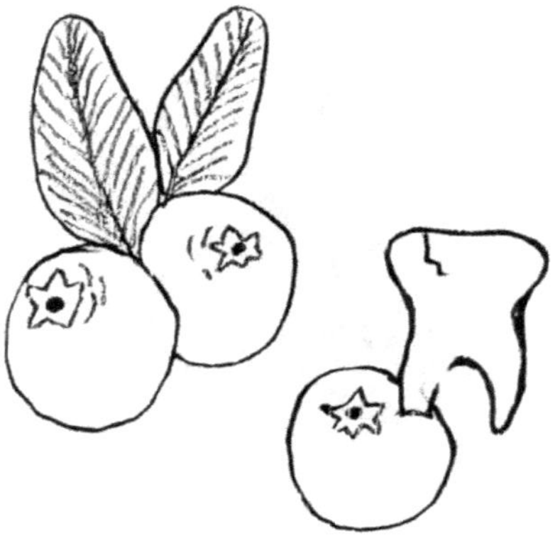

crawling far ahead,
kingdom of undead
wreaks fright,
sparks an eerie dread,
the virus widespread
despite
inhuman they bled,
the fresh flesh instead
they bite.

New Moon

from the oak branch, the fool, the hanged
man dangles, a jester of a man
hanging from his feet; sweet as pecan
pie, he releases and resets, panged
by remorse, as it fell, he ran
from the oak branch.

illusion evaporates, the fanged
beast hibernates; sacrifice to ban
the old and embrace the new, rather than
mining jade. rooted wisdom harangued
from the oak branch.

A Merry Menace

crimson blood cascades from her crown
of cullinan diamonds that shout
her brutal slayings in the town,
so religious and so devout,
so many corpses she might miscount
the charred skin that falls with a thud,
from the ashes terror does sprout,
her gaze in the mirror only sees blood.

ominous church bells for the queen renown,
the heir of lethal flames her father tout,
ruby droplets adorn her satin gown
in which she must fatally scout

her next victim to relieve her drought,
pleas and prayers to the palace flood
through to the queen who wears a pout,
her gaze in the mirror only sees blood.

the queen eternally looks down
on anyone with a sliver of doubt,
her name permanently carves a frown,
chant it thrice alone in the blackout,
stale air heavy with fear throughout
peasants that could not ever sling mud,
violence the queen never went without,
her gaze in the mirror only sees blood.

in the latrine the lights went out,
a chant that some claim is simply a dud,
yet as water dribbles from the spout,
her gaze in the mirror only sees blood.

Basil Gleam

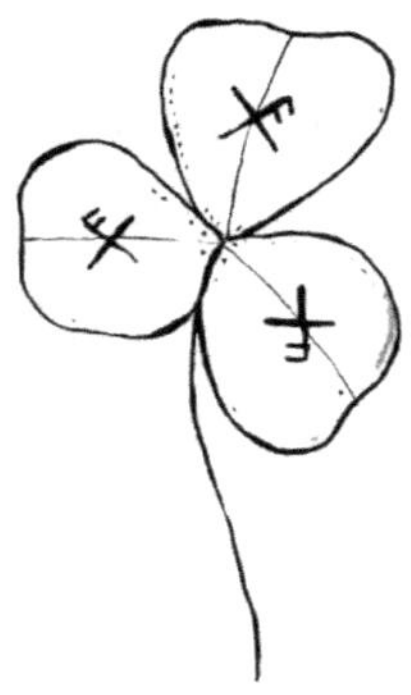

find a penny on the cold asphalt,
pluck a shamrock from the mossy earth
and hope to god the luck fails to rot.
every rainbow ends
two ways,
he marches with a duet of feet,
with shoes crafted by a pair of hands,
lucky number two, please.
sealed in twenty-four karat gold
with an Irish kiss,
but with an Irish twist,
little footsteps grow nearer
a small bout of laughter,
a human down on his luck is a creature
crowned with new treasure.

Expired Wine

weeping willows tremble as the wail
pierces through the sky ever so wary,
her blood-chilling scream did not just entail
the unearthly song from a common fairy,
no, he pours one last glass of sweet sherry;
his finest twill kilt he must now adorn,
her distant shriek he ignored was to warn
but now his wine glass is filled with sorrow,
he falls to his knees with time gone to mourn,
her scream ends as she steals his tomorrow.

Black Death

illuminated by the dark shadow,
she knows tonight her story concludes,
her course of action is simply to be
still before the skeleton in the black robe.

pondering the velvet darkness
that so quickly caresses her in its embrace,
a man of deeper darkness appears,
illuminated by the dark shadow.

she clasps her hands together, trembling,
she feels herself melting into the dark,
she cries and prays and shouts to the moon,
she knows tonight her story concludes.

a scythe reflects moonlight onto her skin,
a shiver creeps all the way down her spine,
her gaze meets his inky eyes, she knows
her course of action is simply to be.

plagued by fear simmering for far too long,
she accepts the hand extended from darkness,
she trembles, so cold, before she goes
still before the skeleton in the black robe.

Waxing Crescent

masquerade mask covering the
face, yet still he sees lightning tower
above; slate clouds gather at the hour
of brutal descent to River Lerma,
remove what is now a sour
masquerade mask.

he falls from Myanmar to Burma,
in the rain and rust he starts to cower
but it is too late to scour
who he is, so he removes the derma
masquerade mask.

Stroll Through a Cemetery

candles flicker out
and thick silence bleeds into the air,
a reprieve,
a reprieve too good to be true
this foggy night.
and too good to be true it is.

crack, crack,
vertebrae searching for a spine,
a femur scouring for a pelvis.
crows sing for death ordinarily
tonight they sing for something more sinister,
a rebirth of sorts,
without the organs
without the skin
without the soul,
crack, crack, crack,
a sea of white floods the cemetery
just before she felt something near her neck,
crack.

The Devil is in the Details

a life sober of desire
she bid an ominous farewell,
tiptoeing into the fire
lit in the foreboding hotel,
her room no more than a cell,
darkness engulfed by the bright flame
embers tell the story of hell
a heart impossible to maim.

the heat making matters dire,
though not sick she is quite unwell
so much so she does require
a deal for her soul she must sell

without a doubt or time to dwell
on the honor of the burnt claim,
sinister tragedy befell
a heart impossible to maim.

the bellhop truly a liar,
shadows of fire do foretell
pain woven throughout the choir
that carols of an aching spell,
easier to sing than to tell,
the horrors of life put to shame
by the smoke her room did expel,
a heart impossible to maim.

ashes coat her skin like a shell,
Lilith rises again in vain,
even darkness cannot dispel
a heart impossible to maim.

Heirs of Darkness

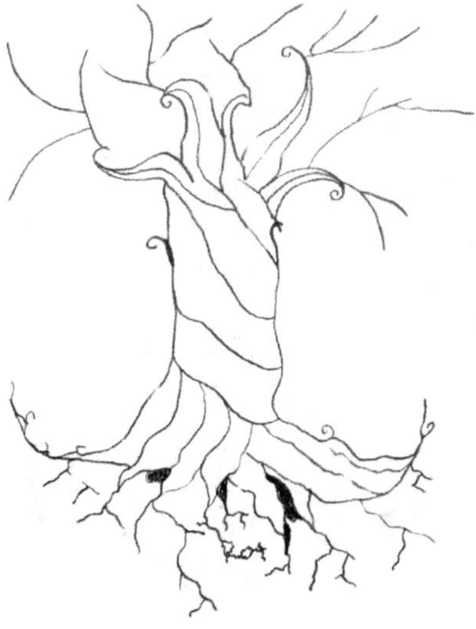

the echo of donkey hooves falls
on deaf ears that strain to obey
the human instinct to delay
an assent of darkness that calls,
a hunger for the flesh of the beast
charred by the fire of the feast,
an appetite unbearable,
morals no longer wearable,
starving for those who are deceased.

First Quarter

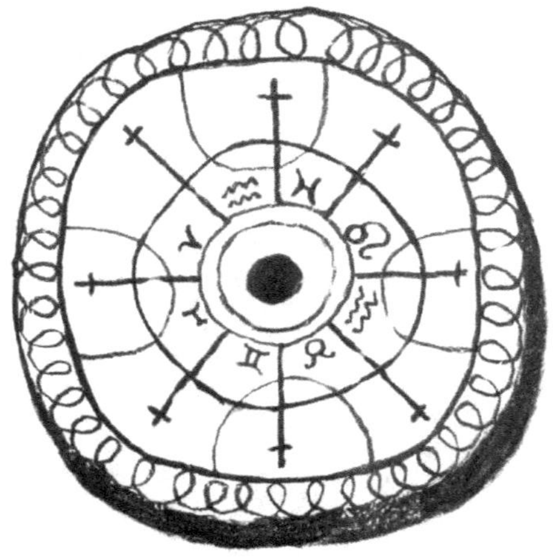

as seasons dance in a group of four,
she governs the gold pentacles
that she relevés on like sentinels
to her own wealth, at a Taurus core
she is young and strong as denticles
as seasons dance.

billowing clouds create before
her magnificent spectacles;
as octopus is to tentacles
she is to wealth, a bud from a spore
as seasons dance.

Heads or Tails?

a copper penny with two tails
predicts a journey where he fails
to miss the cannonball,
his head takes quite a fall,
behind the horseman fresh blood trails.

King of the Green Gnomes

gobble down the last remnants of the meal,
quickly, for hideous laughter echoes and
footsteps that resemble
a raccoon,
a trickster,
a fool
footsteps echo.
a snicker from the posterior
masks a theft from the anterior;

just a hop,
skip,
and an ugly grin away.

When to Go

I am unsure when to go
further or falter mid stride,
when human and beast collide,
I am unsure when to go.

further or falter mid stride
on this path of succumbing
to the costs that are coming,
further or falter mid stride.

on this path of succumbing
to the wild shredding inside,
or to tame I must decide
on this path of succumbing.

to the wild shredding inside
my heart, no wound can compare,
so I give a quick prayer
to the wild shredding inside.

I am unsure when to go
further or falter mid stride,
when human and beast collide,
I am unsure when to go.

Waxing Gibbous

it comes around fast like a Porsche wheel,
though not at speed with his fortune
which dwindles faster, but this distortion
will never mysteriously conceal;
whether it was his potion or portion,
it comes around.

after he recites his appeal,
he spins the wheel of misfortune,
lands on the desire for extortion,
so the wheel spins faster, he tries to steal-
it comes around.

Depth of Darkness Unknown

the god
of underworld,
depth of darkness unknown,
an angel kidnapped by the dark
kidnaps.

Found at Sea

the water lapping at his feet
begs him to swim out even more,
for past the water at the shore,
she would be his pretty defeat.

she sings as his heart fills with heat

so intense, it calls to just him
and him alone, his chances slim,
but he follows her sugar call,
a beautiful demise to all
whose ears her voice happens to skim.

Season of the Witch

autumn trees quiver with fear
in the wind snaking through goosebumps,
the crows overhead shriek
at the girl standing above the rest.
no,
the crows shriek at the rope

now caressing her neck.
with glowing eyes of amber
in the pungent darkness
of the chaotic crowd
she releases one last sigh,
her last breath goodbye,
salem.
the seasons will change,
her bones remain
above the earth she tends to
in darkness and light.
she dances away with the moon;
after all,
tis the season of the witch.

Full Moon

his smile lifts her heart ever so high,
she thought she must consult a priestess
for he makes her dream of Thetis,
and he takes his silk to wipe her eyes dry;
while they together write a thesis,
his smile lifts.

she wishes her broken self goodbye,
shadow a momentary prosthesis,

long ago her heart wrote a treatise
to find the one to meet her in the sky;
his smile lifts.